Israel Style Recipes

A Complete Cookbook of Middle-Eastern Dish Ideas!

BY

Julia Chiles

Copyright 2020 - Julia Chiles

OOOOOOOOOOOOOOOOOOOOOOOOOOOOOOOOOO

License Notes

No part of this Book can be reproduced in any form or by any means including print, electronic, scanning or photocopying unless prior permission is granted by the author.

All ideas, suggestions and guidelines mentioned here are written for informative purposes. While the author has taken every possible step to ensure accuracy, all readers are advised to follow information at their own risk. The author cannot be held responsible for personal and/or commercial damages in case of misinterpreting and misunderstanding any part of this Book

OOOOOOOOOOOOOOOOOOOOOOOOOOOOOOOOO

Table of Contents

Introduction 6

   Israeli Herb Omelet with Dips 9

   Israeli Breakfast Shakshuka 12

   Israeli Sabich Breakfast 15

There are so many delicious Israeli recipes for lunch, dinner, side dishes and appetizers, that it may be difficult to choose which one to start with… 18

   Chickpea Sambusaks 19

   Lamb Kebabs 22

   Chicken & Eggplant Pitas 25

   Cheese Khachapuri 28

   Israeli Curry Couscous 31

   Israeli Fennel Soup 33

   Yirakot Salad 35

Butternut Squash Latkes 38

Israeli Hummus & Eggplant Sandwich 40

Eggplant & Parsley Pashtida 43

Beef Moussaka 46

Onion Fish Cakes 50

Israeli Chickpea Hummus 52

Israeli Pumpkin Couscous 55

Israeli Buttermilk & Vegetable Salad 58

Israeli Pepper & Onion Soup 61

Baba Ghanouj 64

Simanim Pomegranate Salad 67

Stuffed Lamb & Pine Nut Eggplant 70

Israeli Eggplant Lasagna 74

Za'atar Spiced Goat Cheese and Beet Dip 77

Roast Pomegranate Chicken 80

Israeli desserts are some of the tastiest in the Middle East. Try one soon… 83

   Levivot (Sweet Fritters) 84

   Chocolate Crembo (Krembo) 87

   Chocolate Israeli Cookie Truffles 90

   Coconut Sachlav 92

   Israeli Stuffed Dates 95

Conclusion 97

Author's Afterthoughts 98

About the Author 99

Introduction

What factors have influenced Israel cuisine?

How can you recreate their dishes in your own kitchen?

Can you source local ingredients that will still allow you to make authentic recipes?

The geography of the Middle East has influenced the cuisine in a large way, so the foods commonly found in the area, like olives, chickpeas and wheat, have played an important role in Israeli cuisine. The dietary laws of Judaism also have an influence. Jewish festivals and holidays, like Passover and Hanukkah, brought about original recipes.

In Israel, the customs for meals also conform to the Mediterranean region. Lunch is a focal meal, rather than only dinner. In addition, hummus, made from chickpeas, is a staple in most Israeli homes. Fresh vegetables and fruits are plentiful in Israel and are served in many creative ways. Vegetables are often used in breakfast recipes.

As the struggle went on to establish the Jewish nation, it affected the diet of the people. The homes were often small and crowded, and many had no refrigerator. Fresh foods were important in their diet. The orchards of Israel produce wonderful citrus fruits, and grocery stores outside Israel sometimes carry oranges and grapefruit that bear stickers that identify them as having been grown in Israel.

Even though there has been controversy surrounding the recipes of Israel, most people agree that they are creative and delicious. Turn the page, let's cook some Israeli dishes…

Israeli Breakfast dishes are a great way to start the day. Here are some of the most popular…

Israeli Herb Omelet with Dips

Breakfast in Israel is an ultimate choice for people who truly love breakfast time. With its eggs, fresh bread and drinks, you will enjoy it completely.

Makes 2 Servings

Cooking + Prep Time: 30 minutes

Ingredients:

- Tomatoes, sun-dried, with feta
- Tahini
- Olives
- Salty cheese, Bulgarian, cubed
- Jam, apricot
- Labneh – drizzle w/oil & sprinkle w/ za'atar
- Bread, fresh
- Orange juice, fresh if available
- Coffee, hot
- For Omelet
- 4 eggs, large
- Chopped herbs, fresh: chives, green onions, cilantro and parsley
- 1 pinch salt, kosher
- 1 pinch pepper, cracked

Instructions:

1. Organize drinks, dips and bread.
2. To prepare omelets, add a tbsp. oil to a sauté pan over med. heat. Add two of the eggs, chopped herbs, kosher salt & cracked pepper to small sized bowl. Combine well. Pour in sauté pan and cook as you prefer. Serve.

Israeli Breakfast Shakshuka

There are many types of shakshuka, but this one is undeniably for breakfast. Serve with a couple slices of bread so the juices can be properly soaked up and enjoyed.

Makes 4-6 Servings

Cooking + Prep Time: 1 hour & 30 minutes

Ingredients:

- 3 tbsp. of oil, canola
- 2 chopped medium onions, yellow
- 1 cored, de-seeded, chopped large bell pepper, green
- 1 cored, de-seeded, chopped jalapeno pepper, large
- 7 chopped garlic cloves
- 1/4 cup of tomato paste, low sodium
- 1 x 28-oz. can of whole tomatoes, peeled, crushed
- 1 bay leaf, medium
- 2 & 1/2 tbsp. of sugar, granulated
- 1 & 1/2 tbsp. of salt, kosher
- 1 tbsp. of paprika, sweet
- 1 tbsp. of cumin, ground
- 1 & 1/2 tsp. of pepper, ground
- 1 tsp. of caraway, ground
- 1/2 bunch of de-stemmed, chopped spinach or Swiss chard
- 8-12 eggs, large

Instructions:

1. Heat oil in large-sized skillet.
2. Add onions. Sauté on med. heat till translucent, 5-10 minutes or so.
3. Add jalapeno pepper and bell pepper. Cook till barely softened, three to five minutes.
4. Add and stir in tomato paste and garlic. Sauté for a couple minutes more.
5. Pour in tomatoes slowly.
6. Add and stir in caraway, ground pepper, cumin, paprika, kosher salt, sugar and bay leaf. Allow the mixture to simmer for 15 to 20 minutes or so.
7. Layer leaves of Swiss chard or spinach over the top.
8. Crack eggs into tomato mixture.
9. Cover mixture. Simmer for about 8-10 minutes, till egg whites are not translucent anymore. Serve.

Israeli Sabich Breakfast

Falafel gets more attention, but sabich is another very popular snack and breakfast food in Tel Aviv. It's filled with creamy hummus, eggs and eggplant.

Makes 4 Servings

Cooking + Prep Time: 1 hour & 35 minutes

Ingredients:

- 1 x 1"-thick sliced eggplant, large
- 3 tbsp. of oil, olive
- Salt, kosher
- Pepper, ground
- 4 eggs, large
- 4 pitas, warmed, whole-wheat
- 1 cup of hummus, prepared
- 1 cup of red cabbage, shredded finely
- Optional: mango hot sauce

Instructions:

1. Preheat oven to 400F.
2. Use oil to brush slices of eggplant. Season as desired. Roast eggplant on cookie sheet till soft and golden-brown, 30 minutes or so.
3. Place eggs in small sized pan. Cover + 1 inch with cold, filtered water. Bring to boil on high heat. Then remove from heat, cover the pan and allow it to sit for 15-18 minutes. Immediately drain. Cover with ice and cold water. Allow to sit for five minutes or so. Peel eggs and slice them thinly.
4. Slice a pita an inch from its top. Open pocket. Then spread 1/4 cup hummus on one side. Add some cabbage, several eggplant slices, a bit of hot sauce if desired and eggs. Wrap the pita pocket in foil. Repeat with remaining pitas. Serve.

There are so many delicious Israeli recipes for lunch, dinner, side dishes and appetizers, that it may be difficult to choose which one to start with...

Chickpea Sambusaks

These sambusaks are served in other places in the Middle East, but they are thoroughly enjoyed in Israel, as well. You can make them with or without eggs.

Makes 11 Servings

Cooking + Prep Time: 2 & 1/4 hours

Ingredients:

- 1 & 1/2 cups of flour, all-purpose
- 1 tbsp. of corn starch
- 1/2 tsp. of salt, kosher
- 1 tsp. of baking powder, low sodium
- 3 tbsp. + 1 tsp. of oil, vegetable
- 1/3 cup of water, warm, filtered
- 1 chopped onion, extra large
- 1 x 15-oz. can of drained, lightly mashed garbanzo beans
- 1/4 bunch of chopped cilantro, fresh
- 1 tsp. of cumin, ground
- 1 tsp. of coriander, ground
- Salt, kosher, as desired
- Pepper, ground, as desired
- To fry: 2 cups of oil, vegetable
- 11 eggs, large

Instructions:

1. Mix water, 3 tbsp. oil, flour, kosher salt, baking powder and corn starch in medium bowl, forming a dough. Cover bowl. Allow it to set for 10-12 minutes.
2. Divide dough in 11 portions. Form them into balls. Roll balls out on floured work surface into five inch circles.
3. Cook onion in 1 tsp. oil in skillet on med. heat till it has browned, 10 minutes or so. Add and stir in beans, cumin, cilantro, coriander, kosher salt & ground pepper till combined well.
4. Heat two cups oil to 350F in deep skillet.
5. Break one egg into custard cup. Cover with wax paper square. Cook in microwave on high for 35-40 seconds. Place 1 & 1/2 tbsp. garbanzo filling onto dough circle. Place cooked egg on filling. Fold dough gently into shape of half-moon. Fold edge over and seal by crimping with a fork. Repeat with remaining dough, eggs and garbanzo mixture.
6. Deep fry sambusaks, a couple at once, in hot oil till golden brown in color, three minutes or so for each side. Remove and drain on layers of paper towels. Serve.

Lamb Kebabs

These Israeli lamb kebabs are so simple to make, and they will please everyone at your dinner table. They can be made into a wonderful treat for family and friends.

Makes 12 Servings

Cooking + Prep Time: 1 hour + overnight marinating time

Ingredients:

- 2 steaks, lamb, 1" cubed
- 1/4 cup of oil, olive
- 4 minced garlic cloves
- 1 lemon, juice & zest only
- 1 tbsp. of chopped oregano, fresh
- 3/4 cup of yogurt, Greek
- 1 grated, squeezed dry cucumber, small
- 2 tbsp. of chopped dill, fresh
- 1/2 pint of tomatoes, cherry
- 1 x 1" cubed zucchini, medium
- Salt, kosher
- Pepper, ground

Instructions:

1. Combine lamb with 2 tbsp. oil, 3 tsp. garlic, lemon juice & zest and oregano in zipper top plastic bag. Then marinate the steaks in your fridge for one hour minimum, or overnight.
2. Mix yogurt, dill cucumbers and 1 tsp. of garlic in medium bowl. Salt as desired and set the bowl aside.
3. Prepare grill for med-high heat level.
4. Toss zucchini and tomatoes with 2 tbsp. oil. Thread skewers by alternating lamb, zucchini and tomatoes. Sprinkle all sides using kosher salt & ground pepper.
5. Grill lamb till med-rare. Turn occasionally while grilling for 8-10 minutes or so. Serve kebabs with yogurt sauce.

Chicken & Eggplant Pitas

If you've ever had this dish, your mouth may be watering at seeing the recipe again. It is served at small events and for many families and their friends.

Makes 6 Servings

Cooking + Prep Time: 50 minutes

Ingredients:

- 2 x 1/2" sliced eggplants
- 1 tbsp. of salt, kosher
- 2 x 6-oz. halved chicken breasts, boneless, skinless
- To dust: flour, all-purpose
- 2 beaten eggs, large
- 1 cup of breadcrumbs, seasoned
- 4 tbsp. of oil, olive
- 3 peeled garlic cloves + more, as desired
- 2 tbsp. of vinegar, red wine
- 2 tbsp. of oil, olive
- 1 x 12-oz. jar of sliced red peppers, roasted
- Salt, kosher, as desired
- Pepper, ground, as desired
- 6 x 6" pita breads

Instructions:

1. Sprinkle kosher salt over eggplant slices. Allow to drain in colander for 18-20 minutes. Preheat your grill for a med-high heat level.
2. Pound the chicken breasts in between two cling wrap sheets to 1/4" thickness. Dredge them with flour and shake off any excess. Dip them into the beaten egg. Coat with breadcrumbs by pressing into them.
3. Heat 2 tbsp. oil in skillet on med-high. Add the chicken breasts. Cook till golden brown in color and set them aside.
4. Wipe the eggplant dry using paper towels. Brush the slices with 2 tbsp. oil. Grill till well-marked and tender.
5. Crush the garlic. Whisk it together with oil and vinegar. Slice eggplant in strips. Toss them with peppers and dressing. Season as desired.
6. For assembly, heat the pita breads on grill till marked and hot. Slice the chicken in strips. Place in warmed pitas with peppers and eggplant. Serve.

Cheese Khachapuri

These flatbreads are filled with tasty melted cheese, then topped with runny eggs. It's best when you eat it hot, and you can tear off crusts of the flatbread to dip in the cheesy eggs.

Makes 4-6 Servings

Cooking + Prep Time: 2 hours & 20 minutes

Ingredients:

- 1 tsp. of dry yeast, active
- 1/4 tsp. of sugar, granulated
- 1 tbsp. of oil, olive + extra to grease
- 1 & 1/4 cup of flour, all purpose, + extra to dust
- 1 tsp. of salt, kosher
- 14 ounces of Muenster cheese shreds
- 6 ounces of feta cheese crumbles
- 2 eggs, large
- 4 tbsp. of cubed butter, unsalted

Instructions:

1. Heat 2/3 cup of filtered water to 115F. Combine yeast and sugar into water in medium bowl. Allow to sit till it foams, 8-10 minutes or so.
2. Add the oil, all-purpose flour and kosher salt. Mix with spoon till you have a soft dough. Transfer to floured work surface. Knead till elastic and smooth, four minutes or so. Transfer to greased bowl. Loosely cover with cling wrap. Set bowl in warm place till dough size doubles, 45 minutes or so.

3. Place pizza stone on rack in the lower 1/3 of your oven. Heat the oven to 450F for one hour. Combine the cheeses in medium bowl and set it aside.
4. Punch dough down. Divide into halves. Roll 1/2 of the dough into 1/8-inch thick, 10-inch circle on floured baking paper.
5. Spread 1/4 cheese on dough. Leave 1/2-inch border around cheese. On first side of circle, roll dough tightly 1/3 of way toward middle. Repeat on opposite end. Pinch open ends together. Twist and seal into shape like a boat. Place next 1/4 of cheese in center. Repeat these steps with the remainder of dough & cheese.
6. Transfer the boats from baking paper to oven stone. Bake till golden-brown in color, 14 to 16 minutes. Crack an egg in center of all boats. Return to the oven till egg has set a bit, three to four minutes. Put 2 tbsp. of butter on all breads. Serve them hot.

Israeli Curry Couscous

This dinner is a wonderful way to offer guests a side for your protein-packed main dish. Israeli pearl couscous soaks up sauce perfectly and enhances many main dishes.

Makes 8 Servings

Cooking + Prep Time: 25 minutes

Ingredients:

- 2 tbsp. of oil, olive
- 1/4 cup of onion, minced
- 2 cubes of bouillon, vegetable
- 1 tsp. of curry powder, yellow
- 1/2 tsp. of oregano
- 2 cups of Israeli (pearl) couscous
- 2 & 1/2 cups of water, filtered

Instructions:

1. Heat the oil in sauce pan on med. heat. Add oregano, curry powder, bouillon cubes and onion. Break up the bouillon cubes as mixture cooks till onion softens, five minutes or so. Add the couscous. Mix well.
2. Add the water to pan. Bring to boil. Cover. Reduce the heat level to low. Then simmer, while frequently stirring, till the couscous softens, 8-10 minutes or so. Serve.

Israeli Fennel Soup

My family enjoys fennel a lot, so this is a commonly served dish. It's a great choice for serving with rich vegetables dishes, or fish or chicken.

Makes Various # of Servings

Cooking + Prep Time: 1 hour & 10 minutes

Ingredients:

- 3 sliced fennel
- 2 tbsp. of oil, olive
- 1 sliced onion, medium
- 2 garlic cloves
- 1 tsp. of sumac, organic
- 1 cup of wine
- 6 cups of broth or water, filtered
- 2 tbsp. of basil, dried or fresh

Instructions:

1. Sauté onions in oil till their color is light.
2. Add fennel. Continue sautéing till softened lightly.
3. Add garlic and spices. Mix till vegetables are coated well.
4. Add broth or water, then wine. Bring to boil.
5. Reduce heat to med-low. Allow mixture to cook fully through, 40-45 minutes.
6. Add the basil. Blend everything till smooth. Heat and serve.

Yirakot Salad

This is a testy salad, even if you don't have red peppers in the house – they can be left out without affecting the taste much. The flavors are enjoyable, especially if you like sumac.

Makes 4 Servings

Cooking + Prep Time: 1 hour & 5 minutes

Ingredients:

- 2 diced tomatoes
- 2 diced bell peppers, green
- 1 diced bell pepper, red
- 1/2 diced cucumber
- 1/2 cup of oil, olive
- 1/2 diced onion, red
- 2 chopped scallions
- 2 tbsp. of lemon juice, fresh
- 1 tbsp. of parsley, chopped
- 1 tbsp. of chopped mint, fresh
- 1 tbsp. of chopped dill, fresh
- 2 tsp. of vinegar
- 2 minced garlic cloves
- 1/2 tsp. of sumac, ground
- Salt, kosher, as desired
- Pepper, ground, as desired

Instructions:

1. Combine the peppers, tomatoes, oil, cucumbers, scallions, red onions, lemon juice, mint, parsley, vinegar, dill, sumac, garlic, kosher salt & ground pepper in large sized bowl. Mix well.
2. Chill the mixture till flavors have combined, 25-30 minutes. Serve.

Butternut Squash Latkes

These latkes are gluten-free, and they are crispy outside and soft inside. They have so much flavor on their own that you really don't need toppings.

Makes 8 Servings

Cooking + Prep Time: 50 minutes

Ingredients:

- 1/2 peeled, de-seeded butternut squash
- 1/2 finely chopped onion
- 1/2 chopped, de-seeded chili pepper
- 2 chopped scallions
- 1/2 cup of crumbled cheese, Bulgarian if available
- 2 beaten eggs, large
- 3/4 tsp. of pink Himalayan salt
- 1/2 cup of oil, olive

Instructions:

1. Grate butternut squash. Add it and the onions into strainer. Squeeze out excess liquid by hand.
2. Place mixture in a bowl. Add remainder of ingredients except oil. Combine well.
3. Prepare large sized skillet over high heat. Next, add 1/2 cup oil. Heat for a minute or two.
4. Prepare mixture in your palms to create thick, small latke.
5. Cook latke till browned on each side and serve.

Israeli Hummus & Eggplant Sandwich

This is a messy dish, but it's SO tasty it's worth it! It's made with pitas, hummus and vegetables, all put together to create a wonderful veggie sandwich.

Makes 4 Servings

Cooking + Prep Time: 1 hour & 10 minutes

Ingredients:

- 1 baking potato, large
- Salt, kosher
- 1 x 1/2"-thick sliced eggplant, medium
- 3 tbsp. of oil, olive, + extra to brush
- 1 peeled, then halved & de-seeded, diced cucumber, medium
- 1 diced tomato, large
- 1 minced jalapeño, large
- 2 minced cloves of garlic
- 3 tbsp. of cilantro, chopped
- 2 tbsp. of parsley, chopped
- 2 tbsp. of lemon juice, fresh
- Pepper, ground
- 4 warmed pita breads, thick
- 1 cup of hummus, prepared
- 1/4 cup of tahini, organic
- 4 sliced eggs, hard boiled, large
- 4 thinly sliced dill pickles, small

Instructions:

1. Preheat oven to 425F. Add potato to small sized sauce pan and cover with two inches filtered water. Bring to boil. Cook on medium heat till barely tender, 20 minutes or so. Drain. Allow potato to cool. Peel and slice it 1/4" thick and season using kosher salt.
2. Arrange slices of eggplant on rimmed cookie sheet. Brush each side with oil. Season as desired. Bake for 10-12 minutes till tender and browned.
3. Add tomato, cucumber, garlic, jalapeño, parsley and cilantro to large sized bowl. Toss with 3 tbsp. oil and lemon juice. Season as desired.
4. Cut two inches from side of warmed pitas to make them open pockets. Open gently. Spread hummus on bottoms. Add 1 tbsp. tahini over hummus. Layer eggplant, sliced potatoes, egg and tomato-cucumber salad in pitas. Top with sliced pickles. Serve.

Eggplant & Parsley Pashtida

Pashtida is loosely related to quiche, although it is typically made without any crust. It's a delicious jumble of vegetables and eggs and a nice, hearty main dish.

Makes 4-6 Servings

Cooking + Prep Time: 2 & 3/4 hours

Ingredients:

- 1 cubed eggplant, skin-on
- 3 eggs, large
- 1 tsp. of salt, kosher
- 1 tsp. of oil, olive
- 1 tbsp. of mayonnaise, reduced fat
- 4 heaping tbsp. of Matzoh meal, no sodium
- 1 tsp. of cumin, ground
- 2 tsp. of salt, kosher
- 1/4 cup of chopped parsley, fresh

Instructions:

1. Cube the eggplant. Use salt to sprinkle cubes on a cookie sheet.
2. Allow to rest for 10-12 minutes as oven is preheating to 400 degrees F.
3. Drizzle oil on pan. Roast onions and eggplant for 20-25 minutes.
4. Drizzle oil over mixture. Roast for 25-30 minutes.
5. Combine eggs and mayonnaise, Matzoh meal and spices in large sized bowl.
6. Add the eggplant. Mix gently.
7. Pour mixture into 13" x 9" baking pan.
8. Bake at 400F till firm to touch but still lose a little. Serve.

Beef Moussaka

This moussaka, true to its name, includes layers of eggplants, ground beef and matbucha for an Israeli-style, Greek-inspired dish. It's easy to make, although you'll need a couple hours to pull it all together. It's totally worth it.

Makes 6-8 Servings

Cooking + Prep Time: 2 hours & 10 minutes

Ingredients:

- 3 eggplants, medium
- 3 tbsp. of salt, kosher
- 1/2 cup + 2 tbsp. of oil, olive
- 2 diced onions, medium
- 8 minced cloves of garlic
- 1 & 1/2 lbs. of beef, ground
- 2 tbsp. of tomato paste, low sodium
- 1 & 1/2 tsp. of cumin, ground
- 1 & 1/2 tsp. of paprika, sweet
- 1 & 1/2 tsp. of garlic powder
- 2 eggs, large
- Salt, kosher
- Pepper, ground
- 8 ounces of matbucha, prepared
- 1/2 cup of breadcrumbs, kosher

Instructions:

1. Preheat the oven to 400 degrees F. Prepare baking sheet.
2. Slice eggplant lengthways in 3/4" slices and place on paper towels on baking sheet. Use salt to sprinkle each side of slices. Cover them with paper towels. Allow to sit for 1/2 hour or longer, to release their internal moisture. Pat slices dry with paper towels. Place on parchment paper-lined cookie sheet. Brush with oil.
3. Bake eggplant slices for 20-25 minutes, till they have softened and browned lightly. Remove them from the oven. Allow them to cool.
4. Place 2 tbsp. oil in pan on med-high. After pan becomes hot, add onions. Carefully sauté for three to five minutes. Don't allow them to burn. When onions have started to caramelize, add garlic. Cook till garlic aroma can be smelled, 30 to 60 seconds.
5. Add ground beef. Break into crumbs as it cooks. Add tomato paste & spices. Cook for six or seven minutes. Season as desired and allow to cool. Add eggs. Combine well.

6. In deep pan, begin to assemble moussaka. Start with two or three tbsp. of matbucha. Spread it over bottom of pan. Place single eggplant layer. Cover with 1/2 of ground beef. Cover that with 1/2 of matbucha. Repeat with one more layer of each.
7. Combine breadcrumbs and 1/4 cup oil in small sized bowl. Sprinkle with one pinch salt. Evenly spread mixture over top.
8. Cover dish with foil. Bake for 30-35 minutes. Remove foil. Bake for 15 more minutes till top is golden in color. Remove dish from the oven. Allow to sit for five minutes or longer, then serve.

Onion Fish Cakes

This is a dish somewhat like a crab-cake, but it's a kosher specialty made with white fish. It can be served as a tasty snack or combined with a favorite sauce.

Makes 6 Servings

Cooking + Prep Time: 40 minutes + 1/2 hour sitting time

Ingredients:

- 2 pounds of fillet, white fish (sea bass or similar)
- 2 chopped onions, medium
- 2 cups of chopped parsley, fresh
- 1 tsp. of oil, olive
- 1 tsp. of salt, sea

Instructions:

1. Preheat the oven to 450 degrees F.
2. Pulse fish in your food processor. Fish needs to be chopped well, in chunks.
3. Combine all the ingredients in a medium mixing bowl. Allow to sit for 30 minutes.
4. Roll mixture into small-sized balls.
5. Bake in 450F oven for 10-12 minutes. Turn after five minutes. Serve.

Israeli Chickpea Hummus

Hummus is popular world-wide now, flavored with herbs, peppers and more. The Israeli version more likely is made with tahini, chickpeas and paprika.

Makes 4 Servings

Cooking + Prep Time: 1 hour & 20 minutes + overnight chilling time for chickpeas

Ingredients:

- 1/2-lb. of chickpeas, dried
- 1 tbsp. of baking soda, pure
- 7 unpeeled cloves of garlic, large
- 1/2 cup of oil, olive
- 1/4 tsp. of cumin, ground + extra for garnishing
- 1/2 cup of tahini
- 1/4 cup + 1 tbsp. of lemon juice, fresh
- Salt, kosher
- To garnish: paprika, sweet
- 1/4 cup of parsley, chopped
- To serve: pita bread

Instructions:

1. Add chickpeas and two inches filtered water in medium sized bowl. Add and stir in baking soda. Refrigerate chickpeas overnight. Drain, then rinse in cold water.

2. Transfer chickpeas to sauce pan. Cover with fresh water plus two inches. Add cloves of garlic. Bring to boil. Simmer on med-low till chickpeas become tender, 40 minutes or so. Drain and reserve 10 tbsp. cooking water + 2 tbsp. chickpeas. Rinse chickpeas in cold water and peel cloves of garlic.
3. Puree chickpeas with 1/2 cup reserved cooking water, 1/4 cup oil & 6 cloves of garlic in your food processor.
4. Add cumin and 1/4 cup of lemon juice and tahini. Process till you have a creamy texture. Season as desired. Transfer to large bowl.
5. Clean food processor. Add last 1/4 cup oil, 1/4 cup tahini, 2 tbsp. reserved water, 1 tbsp. lemon juice & clove of garlic. Puree.
6. Make well in middle of hummus. Spoon in lemon-tahini mixture. Sprinkle paprika and cumin on hummus. Garnish using whole chickpeas & parsley. Serve with warmed pita bread.

Israeli Pumpkin Couscous

Israeli couscous are tiny nuggets made from wheat or semolina flour and they resemble pasta closely. You'll enjoy the slight nuttiness of its taste in this dish, paired with pumpkin for a perfect fall dinner.

Makes Various # of Servings

Cooking + Prep Time: 50 minutes

Ingredients:

- 2 cups of cubed pumpkin
- 2 tsp. of oil, olive + extra to drizzle
- 2 or 3 minced garlic cloves
- 2 & 1/2 tbsp. of yeast, instant
- 2 cups of couscous, cooked
- 1/2 tsp. of turmeric, ground
- 1/2 tsp. of cumin, ground
- 1/2 tsp. of sugar, brown
- 1 cup of small-diced pepper, red
- 1/2 tsp. of salt, kosher, +/- as desired
- 1/2 cup of pumpkin seeds
- 1 tbsp. of parsley, chopped
- 1/2 cup of cranberries, dried
- 1/2 cup of pine nuts

Instructions:

1. Cut the pumpkin flesh in one-inch cubes.
2. Add 2 tsp. of oil to skillet over med-high heat and brown the pumpkin on each side.
3. Add the turmeric, garlic, sugar, red pepper and cumin. Simmer till the pumpkin softens, while gently stirring so nothing will burn. You can add a bit more oil if you need to.
4. Add mixture to pre-cooked couscous.
5. Add parsley, salt, nuts, seeds, cranberries & drizzle of oil. Serve.

Israeli Buttermilk & Vegetable Salad

It is sometimes said that everyone who lives in Jerusalem enjoys vegetable salads like these. This one is tossed with buttermilk dressing, and you have to taste it to believe it.

Makes 6 Servings

Cooking + Prep Time: 40 minutes

Ingredients:

- 1/4 cup of oil, olive + extra to drizzle
- 2 minced cloves of garlic
- 2 tbsp. of lemon juice, fresh if available
- 2 tbsp. of vinegar, white wine
- 2 tsp. of mint, dried
- Salt, kosher
- Pepper, ground
- 6 thinly sliced radishes
- 4 diced cucumbers, small
- 3 diced tomatoes, large
- 2 thinly sliced scallions
- 1/4 cup of parsley leaves, torn
- 2 tbsp. of mint leaves, torn, fresh
- 1 large sized naan or thin pita bread, toasted, torn in small pieces
- 1 cup of buttermilk, organic
- 1 tbsp. of sumac, organic

Instructions:

1. Whisk 1/4 cup oil with lemon juice, garlic, dried mint and vinegar in small sized bowl. Season as desired.
2. Toss cucumbers, radishes, scallions, tomatoes, mint and parsley in large sized bowl. Add pita or naan pieces. Drizzle with dressing. Toss and combine well. Allow to stand for five – 10 minutes or so.
3. Add buttermilk. Toss once more. Season as desired. Drizzle salad with oil and sprinkle with sumac. Serve.

Israeli Pepper & Onion Soup

Onions are a very popular recipe ingredient in Israeli dishes, followed by potatoes. Who knew they would taste so wonderful when paired with peppers?

Makes 6 Servings

Cooking + Prep Time: 1 & 1/2 hour

Ingredients:

- 6 peppers, red
- 1/2 cup of oil, olive
- 1 onion, red
- 1 tbsp. of ginger, chopped
- 1 tbsp. of garlic, chopped
- 2 to 3 cups water, filtered
- 1/2 cup of milk, coconut
- 2 to 3 tbsp. of honey, pure
- 1/2 cup of almonds, roasted
- Small amount of kosher salt & ground pepper, as desired

Instructions:

1. Heat oven to 450F.
2. Sprinkle a bit of olive oil on peppers. Roast till they char.
3. Remove the pan from the oven. Add peppers to plastic bag and seal. Allow them to cool for 18-20 minutes.
4. Heat fry pan and 3 to 4 tbsp. olive oil.
5. Chop onion. Cook till it starts browning.
6. Add garlic and ginger to onion. Cook for several minutes.
7. Peel roasted peppers. Chop well. Add to pan. Cook for a few minutes.
8. Add a cup of filtered water. Bring to boil.
9. Blend everything together with hand blender till your pepper puree is smooth.
10. Add coconut milk. Season as desired.
11. Bring back to boil. Add water if you need it.
12. Sprinkle on almonds and serve.

Baba Ghanouj

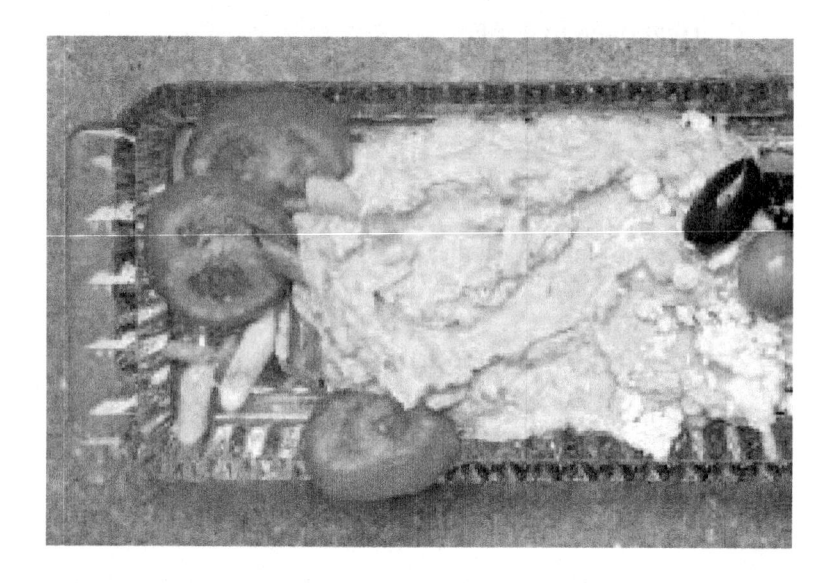

This is a Middle-Eastern, creamy eggplant dip that is often served with warm pitas. In this recipe, you'll top pitas with dip plus a mixture of romaine and tasty veggies.

Makes 4 Servings

Cooking + Prep Time: 55 minutes

Ingredients:

- 2 peeled, cubed eggplants, large
- 3 tbsp. of oil, olive
- 3/4 tsp. of salt, kosher
- 1/2 tsp. of pepper, ground
- 8 pitas, soft
- 1 fresh lemon, juice only
- 1/3 cup of tahini, low sodium
- 3/4 tsp. of cumin, ground
- 2 peeled garlic cloves
- 1 x 1" strip-cut head of lettuce, romaine, small
- 1 lengthways halved & crossways strip-cut tomato, plum
- 1 peeled, lengthwise-halved, de-seeded, thinly sliced cucumber
- 1/2 tsp. of vinegar, wine

Instructions:

1. Heat oven to 450F.
2. Place cubed eggplant on large cookie sheet. Toss with two tbsp. oil + 1/4 tsp. each kosher salt & ground pepper. Arrange cubes in one layer. Stir occasionally while roasting till golden and soft, 13-15 minutes or so. Set them aside for cooling.
3. Reduce oven to 350F. Wrap pitas in foil, a total of two packets each with four pitas. Warm in oven for 8-10 minutes or so.
4. Put eggplant, tahini, lemon juice, garlic, cumin & 1/4 tsp. kosher salt in food processor. Push puree button and puree till you have a smooth texture.
5. In medium-sized stainless steel or glass bowl, combine cucumbers, lettuce and tomatoes. Add vinegar and 1 tbsp. oil. Add 1/4 tsp. each kosher salt & ground pepper. Toss and combine well. Spread some of this baba ghanouj onto pitas. Serve.

Simanim Pomegranate Salad

Each year, cooks try to find different types of recipes for the simanim. What's most interesting is that the most popular simanim foods combine so well in a flavor-filled salad!

Makes 4 Servings

Cooking + Prep Time: 1 hour & 50 minutes

Ingredients:

- 1/2 cup of black-eyed peas, fresh or canned
- 4 oz. lettuce, butter
- 1 leek with chopped white part
- 1 peeled, chopped gourd
- 1 peeled, chopped carrot
- 1/2 peeled, thinly sliced beet
- 1 pomegranate with removed seeds
- 6 pitted, sliced dates
- 1 chopped apple
- 1/2 cup of oil, olive
- 1/2 cup of vinegar, balsamic
- 2 tbsp. of honey, pure
- 1 tsp. of salt, Pink Himalayan or your choice of type

Instructions:

1. Preheat the oven to 375F.
2. Place peas in a small sized pot. Pour water to cover generously. Boil over high heat for 35 to 40 minutes, till peas are soft. Don't let them get mushy, though. Rinse peas and drain.
3. Prepare cookie sheet and baking paper. Add carrots, leeks and gourd. Drizzle with four tbsp. oil. Add 1/2 tsp. of salt. Combine well. Place in the oven for 30-35 minutes, till golden in color.
4. Add the remaining oil, along with vinegar, remaining salt and honey in jar. Combine well.
5. Add lettuce, beets, pomegranate, apple slices and dates to large sized bowl. Add the leeks, carrots and gourd.
6. Mix salad with the dressing and serve at room temperature or warm.

Stuffed Lamb & Pine Nut Eggplant

In this tasty recipe, the halved eggplants will be stuffed using a very flavorful mixture made from lamb, feta cheese and complimentary spices. Pair it with crusty bread and a salad for a tempting meal.

Makes 4 Servings

Cooking + Prep Time: 1 & 1/2 hour

Ingredients:

- 4 x 1-lb. lengthwise-halved eggplants
- 1 tbsp. oil, olive + extra to brush
- Salt, kosher
- Pepper, ground
- 1 tbsp. of cinnamon, ground
- 1 & 1/2 tsp. of cumin, ground
- 1 & 1/2 tsp. of paprika, sweet
- 1 finely chopped onion, large
- 1 lb. of lamb, ground
- 3 tbsp. of pine nuts
- 2 tsp. of tomato paste, low sodium
- 1/4 cup of parsley, chopped
- 1 tbsp. of sugar, granulated
- 1 tbsp. of lemon juice, fresh
- 1 tsp. of concentrated tamarind
- 1 x 1 & 1/2" stick of cinnamon

Instructions:

1. Preheat oven to 425F. Arrange eggplants in large sized casserole dish with the cut sides facing up. Brush them with oil. Season as desired. Bake in top 1/3 of oven for 20 minutes or so, till browned nicely.
2. In small sized bowl, mix cinnamon, paprika and cumin. Heat 1 tbsp. oil in large sized skillet. Add onion and 1/2 of spice mixture. Cover skillet. Cook on med. heat and stir several times till softened well, seven minutes or so.
3. Add lamb to skillet. Break up meat as it cooks till there is no pink remaining, usually four minutes or so. Pour all but 1 tbsp. of fat from skillet. Add and stir in tomato paste, pine nuts, 1 tsp. sugar and 1/2 of parsley. Season lamb as desired.
4. Spoon filling on eggplants. In bowl with remainder of spice mixture, combine a half cup of filtered water, concentrated tamarind, lemon juice, 2 tsp. sugar and 1 pinch each kosher salt & ground pepper. Pour in casserole dish. Add cinnamon stick. Cover dish with aluminum foil. Bake for 45-50 minutes and baste two times with juices in pan, till eggplants are quite tender.

5. Transfer eggplants to platter or plates. Discard stick of cinnamon. Pour juices from pan over eggplants, and sprinkle with the rest of the parsley. Serve.

Israeli Eggplant Lasagna

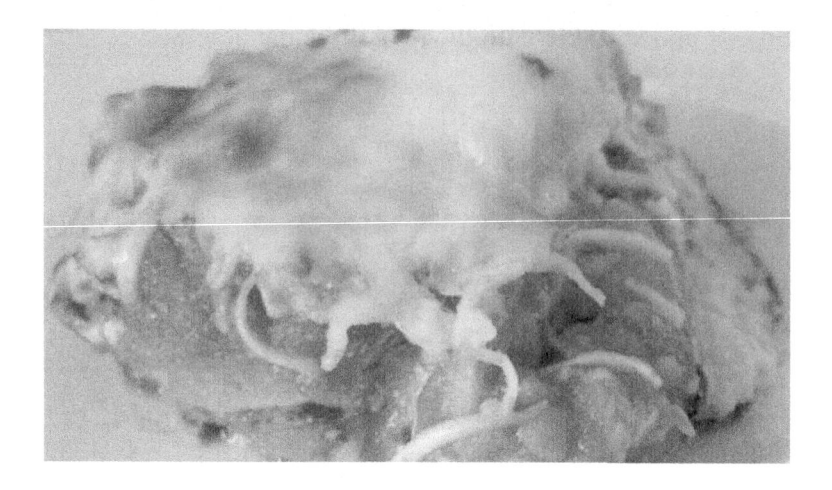

If you're concerned that your favorite foods are not servable during Passover, this will be a welcome recipe. The flavorful cheese, eggplant and tomatoes make a wonderful meal.

Makes 6 Servings

Cooking + Prep Time: 1 & 1/2 hour

Ingredients:

- 1 Matzah packet
- 1 thinly sliced, milk-soaked eggplant
- 1 can of tomatoes, crushed
- 1 chunk-cut onion, medium
- 1 cup of cheese, grated
- Milk, low-fat, to soak matzah – you want it soft but not oversoaked.
- Salt, kosher, as desired
- Pepper, ground, as desired
- Optional:
- Veggies to be added to tomato sauce mixture: 1 pepper and 1 packet of mushrooms, sliced

Instructions:

1. Soak pieces of matzah in low-fat milk.
2. Fry onions gently in pan.
3. Add crushed tomatoes and cut vegetables.
4. Allow to simmer for 15-20 minutes or so.
5. To make lasagna, layer these ingredients in the order listed:
    i. Tomatoes and cut vegetables
    ii. Eggplant slices
    iii. Soaked matzah
6. Continue to layer till you have used all ingredients.
7. Sprinkle the cheese on top.
8. Bake in 350F oven for 40 minutes or so. Serve.

Za'atar Spiced Goat Cheese and Beet Dip

Many ethnic groups in Jerusalem utilize beets a lot in their cooking. In this recipe, beets are pureed and mixed with other delectable ingredients for a popular dip.

Makes 3 cups

Cooking + Prep Time: 1 & 1/2 hour

Ingredients:

- 6 trimmed beets, medium
- 2 minced cloves of garlic, small
- 1 de-seeded, minced red chili, small
- 1 cup of plain yogurt, Greek
- 3 tbsp. of oil, olive
- 1 & 1/2 tbsp. of maple syrup, pure
- Salt, kosher
- 1 tbsp. of za'atar
- 1/4 cup of skinned, chopped hazel nuts, roasted
- 2 tbsp. of crumbled goat cheese
- 2 thinly sliced scallions
- To serve: warm bread

Instructions:

1. Preheat oven to 350F. Place beets in small sized roasting pan. Add 1/4 cup filtered water. Cover with aluminum foil. Bake for an hour or so, till tender. Allow to cool a bit.
2. Peel beets and cut in wedges. Transfer to food processor. Add yogurt, garlic and chili. Pulse till blended well. Add za'atar, oil and syrup. Puree and season using kosher salt. Scrape mixture into shallow, wide bowl. Scatter scallions, hazel nuts and goat cheese over the top. Serve with warm bread.

Roast Pomegranate Chicken

These fragrant, tasty small birds are covered with a glaze of sauce that truly brings out their flavors. They are wonderful when you pair them with potato pancakes.

Makes 8 Servings

Cooking + Prep Time: 2 hours & 10 minutes

Ingredients:

- For the sauce
- 1 cup of sugar, granulated
- 1 cup of pomegranate juice, bottled
- For chicken
- 8 x 1-lb. small chickens (also called poussins) (can use Cornish hens if you like)
- 2 tsp. of salt, kosher
- 2 tsp. of cumin, ground
- 1/2 tsp. of turmeric, ground
- 1/2 tsp. of pepper, ground
- 1/8 tsp. of saffron threads, crumbled
- 3/4 cup of walnuts, roasted
- To fry: 2 tbsp. oil, vegetable, + extra as needed

Instructions:

1. Preheat the oven to 375F.
2. In small sized pan on med-high, whisk 1 cup of water, sugar and pomegranate juice together. Bring to a boil. Leave uncovered and cook for 15-20 minutes, till syrupy and thick.

3. Rinse the small chickens inside & out. Pat them dry. If they still have necks attached, cut them out and discard them.
4. In small sized bowl, whisk kosher salt, turmeric, cumin, saffron and pepper together. Sprinkle over the chickens and press to make sure the mixture adheres.
5. Set a large sized roasting pan over two burners on your stove top. Add 2 tbsp. oil. Heat on med-high till it is hot. Don't allow it to start smoking.
6. Work in two batches to sear the chickens till browned well, five minutes for each side. Transfer when done to large sized platter. Add additional oil if you need it. Return chickens to the pan. Pour the pomegranate syrup on and over the top.
7. Roast chickens for 12-15 minutes. Then baste them with the juices from pan. Scatter walnuts over them. Roast the mixture and baste occasionally till an instant-read thermometer reads 170F, which will take 15-18 minutes or so. Serve.

Israeli desserts are some of the tastiest in the Middle East. Try one soon...

Levivot (Sweet Fritters)

This is a dessert often served for Hanukkah. It is made with tasty fried batter that is topped with an exotic, sugary-sweet syrup. They're simple, but truly delicious.

Makes 24 Servings

Cooking + Prep Time: 1/2 hour

Ingredients:

For levivot

- 1 & 1/2 cups of flour, all-purpose
- 1 tsp. of baking powder, sodium free
- A pinch of salt, kosher
- 1 egg, large
- 1 cup of milk, whole
- To fry: 1 lg. bottle oil, peanut or grapeseed

For syrup

- 3/4 cup of water, filtered
- 1 cup of sugar, granulated
- 1 tbsp. of orange blossom or rose water

Instructions:

1. In medium bowl, mix flour, salt and baking powder together with fork.
2. In separate medium bowl, beat egg. Whisk milk into egg till combined well. Add mixture to flour mixture. Stir, forming batter.
3. Warm the oil on med. heat till sufficiently hot to fry (about 365F).

4. Scoop up batter portions with soup spoon. Drop the batter from full spoons into hot oil. Oil will sizzle but shouldn't splatter. If it does, allow it to cool a bit before continuing. Test one of the levivot first to ensure you have the right temperature.
5. Between spoonful's of the batter, dip spoon into dish with filtered water. This keeps batter from becoming stuck to your spoon.
6. Fry four or five levivot in each batch. Keep a slotted spoon close by so you can be turning them as they are becoming golden brown in color. Fry all sides of levivot and turn once as they fry.
7. Drain the levivot on paper towels after frying.
8. To prepare syrup, combine the filtered water and sugar in small pan. Bring to boil and stir till sugar dissolves. Reduce heat. Simmer liquid lightly for 12-15 minutes while occasionally stirring it. Add the flavoring. Continue simmering for five more minutes till the liquid has thickened. Remove it from the heat. Let it cool a bit.
9. Pour the warm syrup on fried levivot and serve.

Chocolate Crembo (Krembo)

Crembo are made commercially in Israel, and they're a very popular treat. In this home-made recipe, the chocolate-coated confection is made with a cookie base. They are SO good.

Makes 20 Servings

Cooking + Prep Time: 1 & 1/2 hour + 1 hour freezing time

Ingredients:

For the filling (meringue)

- 1/4 cup of water, filtered
- 4 whites from large eggs
- 1 & 1/4 cup of sugar, granulated

For coating (chocolate)

- 10 & 1/2 oz. of chocolate, bittersweet
- 2 tbsp. of oil, neutral

For the base

- 5 & 1/4 oz. of chocolate, bittersweet

Instructions:

1. Lay baking paper on a cookie sheet. Melt the chocolate in double boiler. Spread onto the baking paper. Allow it to sit for three minutes or so, till sheen has disappeared.
2. Cut 1-inch-plus circles from chocolate with glass rim or cookie cutter.
3. To prepare filling, place water and sugar in sauce pan. Bring to boil. Continue to boil for three to four minutes. Beat the egg whites in mixer. Leave the mixer running while using swirling motion to pour sugary syrup slowly into mixer bowl.
4. Fill piping bag with 1/2" round tip with meringue mixture. Swirl onto circles and freeze them for an hour.
5. To prepare coating, melt the oil and chocolate in double boiler. Place frozen crembos gently on rack over large pan. Pour the melted chocolate over each. Freeze till you serve them.

Chocolate Israeli Cookie Truffles

These truffles are a no-bake treat, made from crushed tea biscuits or cookies, chocolate, butter and a little coffee. Rolling them in some powdered sugar Makes them even tastier.

Makes 75 to 80 truffles

Cooking + Prep Time: 25 minutes + 2 hours chilling time

Ingredients:

- 1 lb. of biscuit cookies, chocolate
- 1 cup of butter, unsalted
- 3 & 1/2 oz. of chopped chocolate, bittersweet
- 1 cup of sugar, powdered
- 6 tbsp. of cocoa powder
- 1 tsp. of granulated instant coffee
- 1/2 cup of soy milk or dairy milk

Instructions:

1. Grind biscuits into crumbs in food processor.
2. Place butter and chocolate in top of double boiler over gently simmering water. Stir till they melt. Remove from heat.
3. In large sized bowl, use electric mixer to combine crumbs, melted chocolate, coffee granules and cocoa powder.
4. While still stirring, add milk slowly till batter is sufficiently moist to hold together well when you shape it into balls.
5. Roll mixture in hands into balls the size of walnuts. Roll balls in powdered sugar. Place on plate and cover. Put plate in refrigerator. Chill till firm. Serve.

Coconut Sachlav

If you have a yearning for sachlav, you can make it at home. The creamy drink is thickened with corn starch or rice flour and scented with rose water and vanilla. You can add extra toppings, too, if you like.

Makes 2 Servings

Cooking + Prep Time: 20 minutes

Ingredients:

- 3 cups of milk, coconut or almond
- 1 tbsp. of sugar, granulated
- 2 tsp. of vanilla extract, pure
- 2 tbsp. of corn starch or rice flour
- 1/2 tsp. of rose water
- A pinch salt, sea

For garnishing, any/all

- Cinnamon, ground
- Coconut, shredded
- Pistachios, chopped
- Walnuts, chopped
- Cherries, dried
- Raisins
- Cacao nibs
- Dried figs, chopped
- Dates, chopped

Instructions:

1. Simmer the milk, vanilla bean, sugar, rose water, sea salt and rice flour in small pan on low heat while constantly whisking till thick and hot, usually three minutes or so.
2. Pour into mugs. Let everybody garnish as preferred. Serve.

Israeli Stuffed Dates

This date-based candy is filled with nuts and covered with chocolate. It tastes like you imported it from Israel, and it's sure to be a hit with friends and dinner guests.

Makes 25 Servings

Cooking + Prep Time: 1 hour & 20 minutes

Ingredients:

- 8 oz. of chopped chocolate, bittersweet
- 25 Medjool dates, pitted
- 25 halved pecans
- Optional: 2 tbsp. shredded coconut, sweetened

Instructions:

1. Place chocolate in plastic or glass bowl. Heat in microwave for two minutes or so, while stirring occasionally, till nearly melted. Stir till it is smooth.
2. Line cookie sheet with foil. Stuff dates with 1/2 of a pecan each and place on cookie sheet. Drizzle them with the melted chocolate. Sprinkle using coconut, if desired. Freeze for an hour and serve.

Conclusion

This Israel centered cookbook has shown you…

How to use different ingredients to affect unique Israeli tastes in dishes both well-known and rare.

How can you include Israeli cuisine in your home recipes?

You can…

• Make breakfast Shakshuka or herb omelet breakfasts. They are just as tasty as the ingredients will lead you to believe.

• Learn to cook with Matzah or Matzo, which is widely used by Israeli cooks. Find it in ethnic or Middle Eastern type food markets.

• Enjoy making the delectable seafood dishes of Israel, including carp, whitefish and trout. Fish is a mainstay in the region, and there are SO many ways to make it great.

• Make dishes using tahini and labneh, which are often used in Israeli cooking.

• Make various types of desserts like stuffed dates and cookie truffles that will tempt your family's sweet tooth.

Have fun experimenting! Enjoy the results!

Author's Afterthoughts

Thanks ever so much to each of my cherished readers for investing the time to read this book!

I know you could have picked from many other books, but you chose this one. So, a big thanks for reading all the way to the end. If you enjoyed this book or received value from it, I'd like to ask you for a favor. Please take a few minutes to **post an honest and heartfelt review on** *Amazon.com.* Your support does make a difference and helps to benefit other people.

Thanks!

Julia Chiles

About the Author

Julia Chiles

(1951-present)

Julia received her culinary degree from Le Counte' School of Culinary Delights in Paris, France. She enjoyed cooking more than any of her former positions. She lived in Montgomery, Alabama most of her life. She married Roger

Chiles and moved with him to Paris as he pursued his career in journalism. During the time she was there, she joined several cooking groups to learn the French cuisine, which inspired her to attend school and become a great chef.

Julia has achieved many awards in the field of food preparation. She has taught at several different culinary schools. She is in high demand on the talk show circulation, sharing her knowledge and recipes. Julia's favorite pastime is learning new ways to cook old dishes.

Julia is now writing cookbooks to add to her long list of achievements. The present one consists of favorite recipes as well as a few culinary delights from other cultures. She expands everyone's expectations on how to achieve wonderful dishes and not spend a lot of money. Julia firmly believes a wonderful dish can be prepare out of common household staples.

If anyone is interested in collecting Julia's cookbooks, check out your local bookstores and online. They are a big seller whatever venue you choose to purchase from.

Printed in Great Britain
by Amazon